Egyptian Mythology:

A Guide to Egyptian History, Gods, and Goddesses

Jordan Parr

Table of Contents

Introduction

This book was written to give readers an overview of what life looked like in ancient Egypt and to connect Egyptian culture to ancient Egyptian mythologies. Despite the ancient times they lived in, the Egyptian people were innovative, creative, educational, fair (for most people), and steeped in tradition, ritual, and religion.

However, one of the most important threads that held the tapestry of ancient Egyptian culture together was its mythology, which will be discussed more later on.

There are many things about Egyptian culture and religion that you may be unaware of. For instance, even though there were no practicing traditional doctors, medicine men and women went to school to learn how to brew "potions" (aka medicine or drugs) that would help cure illnesses internally and externally.

Ancient Egyptians were also the first makers of a material very similar to what we know as paper. The papyrus plant gave people a way to write and communicate with one another as well as to write down knowledge for other people.

One of those books was a "herbal remedies" record called the *Ebers Papyrus* and was written in 1500 BCE. It was a combination of over 850 remedies made by those medicinally trained and has survived in good condition to the present day. Some of these formulas are still used today, which include aloe, cedar, coriander, cumin, frankincense, henna, and willow.

And while this book was not the first documented book of medicine and herbal remedies, it does show that ancient Egyptians did add their knowledge to the medical world.

Ancient Egyptian culture can be traced back to 3100 BCE. Before that time, there were two nations, Upper and Lower Egypt. 3100 BCE marks the unification of the two sides of Egypt into one nation.

The history of ancient Egypt is long, colorful, and sprinkled with amazing stories that allow people to get a glimpse of what life was like growing up in Ancient Egypt. While not all was good for the people who lived in this time, their culture and beliefs were what helped them thrive through the heat, sweat, tears, times of war, and more.

The people were separated into four classes. There was the elite (royal and clergy), the middle class, the lower class, and the slave class. This model is similar to many other regions around the world where the wealthy had power while those less fortunate had to work hard to survive.

The people of ancient Egypt were polytheists who believed in many gods and goddesses who would protect the people from famine, floods, and other gods or supernatural beings. The gods could also punish the people if they got out of line or did not give enough homage to the gods and goddesses.

Their reality revolved around these beliefs so much that buildings and structures were created to project the statues of their gods and goddesses. Eventually, these buildings would become so large that they would need over 100,000 people to maintain and keep them. However, only the pharaoh or the high priest was able to see the innermost parts of the complexes.

The pharaoh was known as the child of the gods and therefore considered the mouthpiece of their prophecies, messages, and punishments. The high priest (or priestess) was second in line to perform the duties of the pharaoh if the pharaoh was unable to do so. The priests and other people of the clergy would also clean, keep, and grant offerings to each of the statues.

The statues ranged from popular (national gods) to less worshipped ones (local gods) depending on where the people lived, worked, and what class they were in. National gods and goddesses were subject to larger temples, more offerings, and were around major cities of the elite class. Smaller, state gods were worshipped more frequently by the middle class. Local gods, demigods, and supernatural creatures were worshipped by the lower and slave class of people.

Slaves worked for the royals and elites. Most of the people were there to pay debts to the country, but many people were kidnapped from other places during wars and brought to the palace or temples to work as slaves. These slaves were never (supposedly) treated as such and were given jobs that a butler or maid would do today. They were also fed, dressed, and housed by the royal family. What those clothes, food, and housing looked like for them hasn't been recorded in detail.

Men and women were treated mostly as equals in ancient Egyptian culture. While men did work outside the home and were considered the "head" of the household, women worked inside the home and took care of the family. However, it was also legal for women to sell products, services, and goods without a man around. They could own land and they could divorce their husbands too.

Marriages were also polygamous, which meant that one man could marry many wives. However, there is no record showing that one woman married more than one husband.

Children worked with their parents when they were old enough to. Fathers or uncles would show boys how to do the family business, and girls would learn homemaking skills from their mothers.

In sum, people in all areas and walks of life prayed, celebrated, and performed sacrifices to worship the gods and goddesses and remain in their good graces. This was all in hope of a better life for their people and families.

Chapter One: Life in Ancient Egypt

Ancient Egypt has a culture rich in architecture, education, fashion, flooding, food, jobs, rulers, turmoil, and religion. While their history is well-known due to the amazing documentation from the people of the era, you may still have misconceptions of what life was like in ancient Egypt. While not the main topic of this book, this first chapter will discuss the identity of life in ancient Egypt to give you a better understanding of where people were coming from, where they were going, fashion statements, career paths, and the polytheistic style of their religion.

Ancient Egypt was the civilization that many other civilizations were based upon after Alexander the Great's conquest in 332 B.C. Before that, ancient Egypt unified in 3100 B.C. and ruled an amazing empire for over 300 years. The culture ranges from the Old to the New Kingdom and has captured the world's attention to the point Egyptology has become a studied major in many collegiate institutions.

There are artifacts that archaeologists and scientists are still discovering and identifying to this day, and the items they find are plentiful. These treasures can range from hieroglyphs and art to pottery, jewelry, tombs, and more.

Every artifact reveals another layer of the beauty, culture, and cruelty that encompassed the civilization of ancient Egypt. The picture that emerges is of a culture with few equals in the beauty of its art, the accomplishment of its architecture, and the richness of its religious traditions.

Egyptian mythology came from long ago when Egypt loved more than one god or goddess. Each god or goddess had the power to focus their inventions on one element or entity, like the sun or the river. Plus, they also had their own set of humanistic traits that helped the ancient Egyptians connect to the gods with fear, love, and awe.

As you begin to understand how the ancient Egyptians worked in day-to-day life, you will discover how religion and their mythology could be seen in every part of their daily lives.

Daily Life

The daily life of an ancient Egyptian could range from simple to complex depending on their caste or class. However, many things were normal for anyone throughout the classes. The Egyptian population occupied both sides of the Nile and all had a similar appearance of dark skin and hair.

Whenever they traveled, their main source of transportation would be a boat or a donkey. Donkey transportation and carriage would be the way that anyone from the lower classes would travel if a boat was not accepting work-for-sail riders and they could not pay their way across (or down) the river. The donkey would also be used to carry things long distances.

The river was not only a source of transportation, but a point of supply for the fishing industry. The main source of protein for Egyptians to eat was the fish caught from the river. However, because of the social levels and the ability to pay for fish, not all families had the luxury to eat it.

The most plentiful bounty in Egypt was wheat, which was usually turned into bread. The lower- and middle-class populations would be seen eating bread and drinking beer (barley). Richer families could afford to buy meat, fish, and vegetables. They could also afford to drink wine.

When families from Egypt were cooking, they cooked food in an outdoor courtyard. The people's homes were made from mud to remain cool in the summertime. They also had flat roofs to sleep outside on when it became too hot.

Clothing was a luxury. While most Egyptians wore white to help keep them cooler, not everyone wore shoes. Only the upper class were able to purchase sandals. Men wore robes or skirts, and women wore dresses with shoulder straps or skirts as well. Children often didn't have clothes on at all but did wear jewelry such as necklaces.

Makeup, nail polish, and hair dye were reserved (mostly) for upper class women. They wore red powder on their lips and dyed their hair in many colors. Both men and women were often adorned with makeup, rings, earrings, and other accessories.

Ancient Egyptians had a daily routine of cleansing themselves in the river or at home with water basins. A cleansing cream was made from oils, limes, and perfumes to help them bathe.

While the head of the family was (generally) the husband, no other ancient culture gave the females as many rights as they had in Ancient Egypt. Women could buy and sell land and goods. They could even divorce their husbands.

Although Egyptians were quite innovative and educated in formal trades, only a few school children were taught to read and write (both boys and girls). Mostly these were upper class children who went to special schools to grow up to write official government documents. When not working, the people of ancient Egypt swam, fished, and hunted for sport (and meat).

While the Egyptians had the highest birth rate in the ancient world (from 2600 B.C. to 500 AD), their lives were far from easy. Between sickness, accidents, flooding, and poverty, the chances of living a long life were quite poor.

Social Structure

Their upper, middle, and lower class bears similarities to many social systems still active today. The upper class was the educated and wealthy, such as landowners, religious leaders, the pharaoh, and the pharaoh's family. The middle class was made up of artisans and merchants. The lower class were the people who worked in the farms and fields.

Slaves were also part of the social structure; however, they did not play a role in the caste system. Slaves in ancient Egypt were prisoners taken from conquered and foreign lands.

Although there are split views on the slave structure from ancient Egypt, much of academia has found evidence that suggests that slaves performed more servant roles than actual slave roles. Other scholars believe that slaves were forced to do jobs that would be considered humiliating for anyone else to do. Another group of scholars suggest (which is the most popular idea – even though there is much debate around it) that slaves built the great pyramids.

The pharaoh was in a class of their own. A pharaoh's status gave them the sole ability to speak with the gods and goddesses, thus rendering them invaluable to religious institutions and the citizens of their society. This ability to communicate with the divine made them superior to everyone else.

Besides the caste system, the family was a recognizable support system for everyone. Marriage and family were institutions of vital importance as marriages were chosen based on practical and strategic planning so the family could support each other economically or otherwise.

These unions were never looked at as a romantic gesture. People entered into matrimony for only one reason: support. Even the gods and goddesses were married to connect the idea that family meant stability and a good foundation for living.

Any unmarried man could be seen as incomplete. For example, male school-aged children married early in their lives and fathered as many children as they could.

However, marriages happened in the early teenage years for both males and females who would then start to train in the trades of their families and genders. Most times, males would be trained in their family business and apprentice under their father or uncle while the females would learn how to care for and keep a household from their mothers.

Jobs

The Egyptians had many choices when it came to career opportunities. While many people usually inherited their job from their parents or family, it wasn't necessarily the only path you could take (depending on who you were). Instead of going to college to learn how to do something, they would begin apprenticeships from a young age, which meant that children were learning trades to last their lifetime.

Once a child started an apprenticeship, they generally stuck to it. The Egyptian child would either inherit the position once the expert passed away or no longer could work in the trade, or they would continue to work in the same environment for the rest of their lives.

There were peasants (lower class) throughout the caste system who lived off the land through farming. Farms with wheat were the main staple of ancient Egyptian life, and many in the lower class would have worked on farms to maintain a living for their families.

Because of the ingenuity in Egypt, these people were one of the first to develop and use plows drawn by oxen. Farmers who made a living off of their land would have had a hard time paying the lower class a good wage, as the pharaoh and their people would tax any crops that were farmed, which made moving up through ranks nearly impossible.

Since Egypt had little rainfall, the farmers and their families also depended on the Nile River for water. These farmers brought out other innovations and built canals to bring water from the river to their farms. These farmers also prayed to the gods to get the yearly floods and fertile soils.

Craftsmen all had shops to help them sell their wares. Their main products were bricks, furniture, jewelry, pots, bowls, and textiles. All these items were made by hand or with hand tools, and much of the material was limestone or sandstone found in the mines.

Sailors had a good job because the Nile River was the fastest connection from one side of Egypt to the other. Papyrus boats were made, and they used stick poles to get the ships, sailors, products, and people across the river. Eventually, the sailors evolved and made sailboats.

Traders, another job with a foot hole in the middle class, would sail over the river to countries bordering Egypt to trade local goods and bring back goods from other places. Traders would sail up as far as Southwest Asia to bring back materials like gold, ivory, animal skins, cattle, spices, silver, and wood.

Women

Not all women in the ancient world of Egypt were treated as property or second-class citizens. Many times, they were treated equally to men. Women were allowed to conduct business, own property, and testify in court, just as men could. Egypt even had more than one female ruler.

In general, most women were the primary caretakers of the children and their family's home. The responsibility to oversee a household was their duty.

The married couple did play separate roles in the household. The male worked and provided for his family outside the home, and the wife provided anything the family would need internally. Inside the house, the needs were cleaning, clothing, drinks, educating daughters, and meal planning.

Even though a woman's role inside a home was considered important, Egyptians rarely left written records. Therefore, there is little else known about women besides the legal rights and the oversight of the family home.

Men

Men, as stated above, worked outside the home. They were farmers, field workers, etc. Their main job was to make a living wage that would allow the family to prosper.

Because men were looked upon as the more revered gender, they were taken into servant status when used as a slave. Some of these men would become craftsmen and learn a trade to help pass over the custom to potential offspring.

Children

Egyptians believed that children were a blessing from the gods, especially for the royal family and upper class (nobles). Many artists depict loving touching scenes between kings, queens, and their children.

Family Life

Divorce was a rarity because of how Egyptians viewed the sanctity of marriage. The social system of ancient Egypt required that family life be essential for the entire population. Both men and women would marry young, and men may have had several wives and children. There would be a senior who was married the longest and considered the leader of all other wives in the family.

Architecture

Depending on the status of each family in ancient Egypt, family homes could range from shacks to two or three-story buildings. However, all buildings were made from mud, had windows to keep the domicile cool, and had flat roofing so families could climb up and sleep on top of the house during the hotter months.

But Egypt isn't known for its huts and homes. It is known for the pyramids.

The pyramids were built in the Old Kingdom and are among the oldest structures in the world. While only ninety still stand along the Nile River, the three largest pyramids at Giza are now part of the Seven Wonders of the Ancient World, which means the structure can be seen from space.

The Great Pyramid is about 140 meters high and was built with over 2 million blocks of limestone. Next to it is the Great Sphinx, a masterpiece of Egyptian sculptors. It is a stone statue with the head of a person and the body of a lion.

Fashion

Most of their clothing was made of light and soft linen that was colored in cool dyes to promote comfort and moderate temperatures. The clothes were generally wrapped around or draped over their bodies. The upper class wore sandals that were made from leather and plant fibers. Some also donned their heads with headdresses (mostly associated with pharaohs).

All genders and ages wore makeup. They used coal around their eyes and red powder for their lips. Makeup was not only a fashion statement but helped protect against skin damage from the sun.

Jewelry was a main staple for all Egyptians. They had pierced ears and wore rings, amulets, headdresses, and necklaces. The upper class would go a little further and buy jewelry from beads, pendants, gold, silver, and electrum (a mixture of gold, silver, and other precious metals).

Their hieroglyphics and art tend to paint the Egyptian elite dressed in white with pleated garments, often portraying them as eating, walking through fields, or enjoying a banquet with other decadently dressed elites.

As for daily hygiene rituals, the ancient Egyptians washed their clothes frequently. The clothes were cleaned with natron, which is a cleaning agent made from salt-rich minerals.

Pregnancy and Birth

Regular bathing helped keep the body free from illness and disease, but there was still little medical knowledge. Charms and amulets were given to pregnant mothers to help with the pain of labor and childbirth. These pieces usually had images of the Hippopotamus goddess Taweret, and the dwarf demigod, Bes. The figures of gods and goddesses were used to protect the mother and unborn child.

When ready to give birth, the mother would remove her clothing and let her hair down. She would squat on birthing bricks (stone or brick the mother would squat on for support while the baby was born) for the baby's delivery. A midwife would catch the newborn and then cut the umbilical cord with a flint or obsidian knife.

Complications usually led to the death of the baby, the mother, or both.

Housing and Shelter

Any stones within the city or towns were saved for building temples or tombs. All other standing structures were made from bricks of mud. Due to the heat and weather, homes had to be repaired or even replaced frequently because they would crumble or dissolve.

However, the home of the royal tomb-builders in Deir el-Medina still stands to this day and is mostly intact. The house is terraced with long, narrow dark rooms with wooden doors open to the city's main street. Each house had two living areas, a storeroom, a kitchen, and a bedroom.

The kitchens were outfitted with mud-brick ovens, and the roof (only over the kitchen) was made from matting that would allow ventilation for smoke and cooking smells. To keep food and drinks fresh, they had to dig pits close to or below the ground level where the earth was cooler.

Other furniture inside the house was built into the house so they wouldn't have to move anything. The roof could be accessed by stairs or a ladder and was used as another gathering place.

Farming & Food

Egypt was a land of fertile soil. Normal circumstances of weather ensured that no one went hungry. Many people grew food at home and used rations to eat amongst their families. There was also hunting and fishing. The food caught or killed could be bartered at the markets as there was no form of official currency.

Farms were built with access to the Nile River to build irrigation canals and water their crops. Grain, wheat, or barley was the main carbohydrate that most farmers grew. Even the gods and goddesses ate a lot of bread each day, their temples filled with hundreds of loaves as offerings.

Vegetables and fish were also available and consumed in a healthy diet by the middle- and upper-class levels. As long as the lower-class people could hunt, fish, and farm, they could also eat a healthy meal.

Although there was no poultry in ancient Egypt, the upper class also ate other meats regularly. On top of that, they would also eat figs, grapes, and seasoning. Onions and garlic were grown easily, and there was always a demand for them.

Health

The doctors of ancient Egypt were considered the best in the ancient Mediterranean world. Egyptian doctors observed, diagnosed, and incorporated a ritual of magic with spells and charms in order to treat those who came to them.

Mummification was a specialty of this time. During mummification, the doctors would pull out organs through the deceased's nose, believing that having open canals centered the heart (aka blood vessels, tear ducts, nerves). Anything that obstructed your system could cause issues in other parts of the body.

_Ma'at_'s Importance

Storytelling was an important form of education, spirituality, and entertainment to the Egyptians. All myths started as an oral tradition, which later moved into literature in a later period.

However, no matter what year the first composition of a story was, harmonious balance through _ma'at_ was part of the central theme. It is the one element that remains standard in each myth, symbolizing the disruption of harmony and how each hero would need to restore it.

The Egyptians believed that everything in the universe should be in constant balance. And, because humans were part of the universe, it was their responsibility to also continue in eternal balance. _Ma'at_ was an underlying force that was present even before anything was created. It made all life possible.

Heka was given to the gods and goddesses from the universe. It was a magical power that allowed them to create, sustain, and respond to all life as needed. This magic was also personified by the god Heka who allowed a soul to pass from earth to the afterlife.

As every soul left its body at death, it found its way to the hall of truth. Osiris waited for these souls to pass judgment on them, which would allow them to move onto the Field of Reeds. Osiris judged these souls with a golden scale and the white feather of *ma'at*.

If the soul's heart was lighter than a feather, that soul could go live in purification and eternal bliss. However, if the heart was found to be heavier than the feather, Ammut (the gobbler) would come out of the floor and eat it up. The soul would then no longer exist.

Egyptians did not believe in "hell" as many modern-day monotheistic religions do. Instead, they feared the eternal darkness brought on in the afterlife of someone whose heart was too heavy. The unconsciousness of the afterlife, not in the Field of Reeds, would provide them nothingness, which was considered to be worse than any other existence. Since having your soul move on was part of the universal journey, being separated from that journey and moving into non-existence was much more terrifying a thought than what an underworld of torment could provide them with.

Pharaohs

Pharaohs were the rulers of ancient Egypt. They were the head of state and the religious leaders of all who resided in this time. Pharaoh actually means "great house," which refers to the palace where each pharaoh lived.

Since each pharaoh was also the religious leader of their people, they had the task of maintaining the relationship between the divine and the Egyptians. Maintenance of the divine and people could be difficult as the pharaoh had to attend ceremonies to both keep the religion thriving and the crops plentiful. The position of head of state allowed the pharaoh to make laws, wage war, collect taxes, and oversee the land.

While the hieroglyphics were and are being translated, a large number of scholastic experts believe that Narmer (or King Menes) was the first pharaoh. Narmer was the first ruler, in writing, that united and essentially ruled the upper and lower part of Egypt.

Both women and men could rule as a pharaoh, although they were typically male. A few women like Cleopatra, Nefertiti, and Hatshepsut made names for themselves.

Although very successful as a leader, Hatshepsut, doesn't have monuments or inscriptions about her as the other pharaohs do. Many of her statues, monuments, and hieroglyphics were destroyed after her death. The theory is that by destroying her statues and history, the Egyptian rulers were trying to discourage other women from being future rulers.

In death, pharaohs would be locked into a tomb with a variety of riches they could use in the afterlife. Tutankhamen was one of the more famous pharaohs who has been uncovered. Although he died at the age of nineteen, the archaeologist who discovered his tomb was able to learn a lot about the Egyptian culture from everything in his tomb. Since 1922, archaeologists continue to find more untouched tombs, which allows us to become even more knowledgeable about ancient Egypt than before.

Egyptian pharaohs also had a royal titulary – the standard naming convention that rulers took as they stepped up to rule. The ceremony symbolizes supremacy and holy might. Although many pharaohs had up to five names, many only used one or two of them. These names were altered to mark a significant event during their reigns and could be combined to be labeled as Horus, Golden Horus, Nebty, Throne, along with their birth names.

There were many pharaohs throughout ancient Egypt. See the list below:

Archaic Period

- **(Predynastic)** – all rulers on this list were in charge of Lower Egypt. None of them show up in hieroglyphics more than once, which leads many scholars to question whether these rulers were mythological or real.

    - Seka

    - Khayu

    - Tiu

    - Tjesh

    - Neheb

    - Wenegbu

    - Mekh

- I

    - Narmer – or King Menes, is known for uniting the upper and lower parts of Egypt as it was referred to as "two lands" before this. Scholars can decipher this information because of the names given to him through his reign. *Meni* is a name for "the first." Many similar sources all use this term to name him, making it likely that he is the first true king.

    - Aha

    - Djer

- o Djet
- o Den
- o Adjub
- o Semerkhet
- o Qaa

- **II**
  - o Hotepsekhemwy
  - o Nebra
  - o Ninetjer
  - o Wadjenes
  - o Senedji
  - o Skehemib
  - o Peribsen
  - o Sneferka
  - o Neferkasokar
  - o Hudjefa I
  - o Khasekhemwy

Old Kingdom

- **III**
  - o Nebka
  - o Djoser

- ○ Sekhemkhet
- ○ Hudjefa II
- ○ Mesochris
- ○ Nebkara
- ○ Neferkara
- ○ Huni
- **IV**
  - ○ Sneferu
  - ○ Khufu
  - ○ Radjedef
  - ○ Khafra
  - ○ Menkaura
  - ○ Shepseskaf
  - ○ Baufra
  - ○ Thamphthis
  - ○ Hordjedef
- **V**
  - ○ Userkaf
  - ○ Sahura
  - ○ Neferirkara I
  - ○ Kakai

- o Shepseskara

- o Netjeruser

- o Neferefra Isi

- o Niuserra Ini

- o Menkauhor Kaiu

- o Djedkara Isesi

- o Unas

- **VI**

  - o Teti

  - o Userkara

  - o Pepi I

  - o Nemtyemsaf I

  - o Pepi II

  - o Nemtyemsaf II

First Intermediate Period

- **VII**

  - o This period has no known names of pharaohs. The only information that can attest to it will be Africanus/Eusebius.

- **VIII**

  - o Netjerikara

- o   Menkara
- o   Neferkara II
- o   Neferkara
- o   Neby
- o   Djedkara Shemai
- o   Neferkara Khendu
- o   Merenhor
- o   Neferkamin I
- o   Nikara
- o   Neferkara
- o   Tereru
- o   Neferkahor
- o   Neferkara Pepiseneb
- o   Neferkamin Anu
- o   Qakara Ibi
- o   Neferkaura
- o   Neferkauhor
- o   Neferirkara II

- **IX**

- o   Meribra Khety I
- o   Neferkara III

- o Wahkara Khety II

- o Senen

- o Neferkara Khety III

- **X**

  - o Nebkaura

  - o Khety IV

  - o Merikara

  - o Sekhemkara I

  - o Wadjkara

  - o Ity

  - o Imhotep

  - o Hotep

  - o Khui

  - o Isu

  - o Iytenu

Middle Kingdom

- **XI**

  - o Mentuhotep I

  - o Intef I

  - o Intef II

- Intef III
- Mentuhotep II
- Mentuhotep III
- Mentuhotep IV

- **XII**

  - Amenemhat I
  - Senusret I
  - Amenemhat II
  - Senusret II
  - Senusret III
  - Amenemhat III
  - Amenemhat IV
  - Neferusobek

Second Intermediate Period

- **XIII**

  - Sobekhotep I
  - Sonbef
  - Nerikara
  - Sekhemkara Amenemhat
  - Ameny Qemau

- Qemau Siharnedjheritef
- Iufni
- Sankhibra Amenemhat
- Nebnun
- Sewesekhtawy Sehotepibra
- Sewadjkara
- Nedjemibra
- Sobekhotep II
- Ranisonb
- Hor I
- Sekhemra Khutawy
- Djedkheperu
- Sebkay
- Sedjefakara Kay-Amenemhat
- Wegaf Khendjer
- Imyremeshaw
- Intef IV
- Meribra Seth
- Sobekhotep III
- Neferhotep I
- Sihathor

- o Sobekhotep IV

- o Sobekhotep V

- o Sobekhotep VI

- o Wahibra Jaib

- o Aya Ini

- o Sewadjtu

- o Ined

- o Sewadjkara Hori

- o Sobekhotep VII

- o Merkheperra

- o Merkara

- o Mentuhotep V Ibi

- o Hor II

- o Se...kara

- o Sankhptahi

- o Sekhaenra

- o Maara Sobekhotep

- o Senebmiu

- **XIV**

  - o Yakbim

  - o Yammu

- Qareh
- Aahotepra
- Sheshi
- Nehesi
- Khakherura
- Nebfaura
- Sehabra
- Merdjefara
- Sewadjkara III
- Nebdjefara
- Webenra
    - ...djefara
- Awibra
- Heribra
- Nebsenra
- Sekheperenra
- Djedkherura
- Sankhibra II
- Nefertum...ra
- Sekhem...ra
- Kakemura

- Neferibra
- I...ra
- Khakara
- Akara
- Hapu
- Anati
- Babnum
- Senefer...ra
- Men...ra
- Djed...ra
- Inek...ra
- A...ra
- Ap...
- Wazad
- Shene

- **XV**

  - Salitis
  - Sakir-Har
  - Khyan
  - Apepi
  - Khamudy

- o Aperanat

- o Semqen

- o Apachnas

- o Sharek

- o Beon

- **XVI**

  - o Djehuty

  - o Sobekhotep VIII

  - o Neferhotep III

  - o Mentuhotepi

  - o Nebirau I

  - o Nebirau II

  - o Semenenra

  - o Bebiankh

  - o Sekhemra Shedwaset

  - o Dedumose I

  - o Dedumose II

  - o Mentuemsaf

  - o Mentuhotep VI

  - o Senusret IV

  - o Pepi III

- Nebmaatra
  - Anetjerira
  - Meribra
  - Nubankhra
  - Nikara II
- **XVII**
  - Rahotep
  - Sobekemsaf I
  - Sobekemsaf II
  - Intef V
  - Intef VI
  - Intef VII
  - Senakhtenra
  - Seqenenre
  - Kamose
  - Abydos
  - Senebkay
  - Wepwawet Msaf Panteny
  - Snaaib

New Kingdom

- **XVIII**
    - Ahmose I
    - Amenhotep I
    - Thutmose I
    - Thutmose II
    - Hatshepsut
    - Thutmose III
    - Amenhotep II
    - Thutmose IV
    - Amenhotep III
    - Amenhotep IV
    - Neferneferuaten
    - Smenkhkare
    - Tutankhamun
    - Ay
    - Horemheb
- **XIX**
    - Ramesses I
    - Seti I
    - Ramesses II

- o Merenptah
- o Seti II
- o Amenmesse
- o Siptah
- o Tausr

- **XX**

  - o Setnakht
  - o Ramesses III
  - o Ramesses IV
  - o Ramesses V
  - o Ramesses VI
  - o Ramesses VII
  - o Ramesses VIII
  - o Ramesses IX
  - o Ramesses X
  - o Ramesses XI

Third Intermediate Period

- **XXI**

  - o Smendes I
  - o Amenemnesut

- ○ Psusennes I

  ○ Amenemope

  ○ Osochor

  ○ Siamun

  ○ Psusennes II

- **XXII**

  ○ Shoshenq I

  ○ Osorkon I

  ○ Shoshenq II

  ○ Shoshenq IIb

  ○ Takelot I

  ○ Osorkon II

  ○ Shoshenq III

  ○ Shoshenq IV

  ○ Pami

  ○ Shoshenq V

  ○ Pedubast II

  ○ Osorkon I

- **XXIII**

  ○ Takelot II

  ○ Pedubast I

  - Iuput I
  - Shoshenq VI
  - Osorkon III
  - Takelot III
  - Rudamun

- **XXIV**

  - Tafnakht
  - Bakenrenef

- **XXV**

  - Piye
  - Shabaka
  - Shebitko
  - Taharqa
  - Tenutamen

Late Period

- **XXVI**

  - Necho I
  - Psamtik I
  - Necho II
  - Psamtik II

- Apries
- Amasis
- Psamtik III

- **XXVII**
  - Cambyses II
  - Darius I
  - Xerxes I
  - Artaxerxes I
  - Darius II
  - Artaxerxes II

- **XXVIII**
  - Amyrtaeus

- **XXIX**
  - Neferites I
  - Akoris
  - Psammuthis
  - Neferites II
  - Muthis

- **XXX**
  - Nectanebo I
  - Djedhor

- o Teos I
  - o Nectanebo II
- **XXXI**
  - o Artaxerxes III
  - o Arses
  - o Darius III
- **Argead**
  - o Alexander the Great
  - o Philip III Arrhidaeus
  - o Alexander IV Aegus

Ptolemaic

- Ptolemy I
- Ptolemy II
- Ptolemy III
- Ptolemy IV
- Ptolemy V
- Ptolemy VI
- Ptolemy VII
- Ptolemy VIII
- Ptolemy IX

- Ptolemy X

- Ptolemy XI

- Ptolemy XII

- Ptolemy XIII

- Ptolemy XIV

- Cleopatra VII

- Ptolemy XV[1]

Famous Pharaohs

- Tutankhamu

- Ramesses II

- Amenemhat III

- Thutmose III

- Hatshepsut

- Ramesses III

- Khufu

- Djoser

- Narmer

- Pepi II

- Sneferu

- Cleopatra V

Culture

Throughout the last few centuries, the painting and drawings depict Egyptian culture as its people engaged in fishing, boating, hunting, swimming, and playing games. Other images show people playing hockey or having rowing competitions. These were early-day versions of present-day sports.

Each station (upper, middle, lower) would have its own form of entertainment. The upper class threw extravagant parties with music, food, and drink. Festivals were a common form of entertainment for everyone as well.

Children had toys made from wood or mud that were carved in animal shapes, board games, balls, and other toys with wheels.

The Nile

The Nile River provided an annual flood to help farmers grow their crops and was an essential part of living life in ancient Egypt. The river was a primary water source for drinking, fishing, swimming, irrigation, and more. It also gave people plant life, like papyrus reeds which were used for making paper, and materials for building houses.

Life after Death

Religion and life after death were incredibly sacred to ancient Egyptians and they did not think death was the end of life for Egyptians. They believed they could live again with the help of a preserved, natural body to help bridge the spirit and the living lands.

Once a person passed on, their body was delivered to an undertaker. The undertaker would strip, wash, and embalm the body. They would then begin to remove organs like the brain, stomach, lungs, intestines, and liver. These were all drawn out through a left-flank side incision that left the body empty. The brain was separated from the skull cavity and pulled out through the nostrils (the ethmoid bone that separates the nasal cavity from the skull cavity was broken to do this).

While the heart was left intact and in place, the empty body would then be stuffed with natron salt for preservation. After forty days of drying, the body was then washed, oiled, and wrapped up.

Mummification was reserved for those who could afford the treatment. The majority of people were buried in desert graves.

Religion

Egyptian mythology was the foundation of their ancient religions and science couldn't separate religion from magic at this time. Like the people living during that time, their many deities were arranged in a social hierarchy. Gods and goddesses had national recognition; local gods and goddesses would be in the middle class, and demigods and supernatural creatures were in the lower class.

State religion excluded any peasants or noble persons who weren't the king and priests themselves. Other people would then worship the local gods and goddesses in an eclectic mix of influence, rule, and spirituality.

The supernatural creatures, demigods, spirits, and ancestors of the Egyptian people were imbibed with magic, and they had a great influence on the general public. Other magics were spread throughout all levels of society and religious figureheads. It was the power behind the protection of the innocent and warded them against harm.

Conclusion

Ancient Egyptians lived a full and rich life, particularly if they were lucky enough to have been born in the upper classes. Those who were in the middle, lower, and impoverished classes were less fortunate, but were also always striving for innovation.

Although women generally stayed at home, raised children, and took care of the family, they could legally own land, sell goods at the market, and divorce their husbands. Men were known as the heads of the family and worked outside the home. When their sons were old enough, they would take the boys to work with them to teach them their trade. If the sons weren't interested in their father's work, they could apprentice with brothers or uncles.

Childbirth was painful and protected with amulets that had Taweret and Bes on them. Egyptians believed that these amulets would see the mother and the unborn baby through childhood.

The health, hygiene, and beauty regimen of ancient Egyptians rivals some of the current day trends as they had all genders wearing makeup and took baths or showers every day. Health, while innovative for its time, was still a new practice for doctors. Many brewed up "potions," and relied on magical favors from the gods.

Pharaohs could be both men and women. They had naming rituals and generally held up to five names pulled from experiences within their rule. These titles were called Horus, Golden Horus, Nebty, Throne, and their Birth Name.

Narmer, the king who unified lower and upper Egypt, is known as the first pharaoh of the Two Lands. However, there were notes of other rulers before Narmer, but since they have been infrequently noted historically, scholars are uncertain if this means they were myths or real people.

Religion and life after death intertwined at some points as their mythology was the foundation for ancient Egypt. Deities were arranged in a hierarchy same as the people who lived in the upper, middle, and lower classes. Some gods and goddesses were nationally or locally recognized while demigods and supernatural creatures would be worshipped by the lower classes.

Their belief in life after death allowed for specific types of rituals. Mummification and entombment would allow for the pharaohs to take all items of value with them to the afterlife. Mummification also helped preserve their bodies with incredible detail. Although the same treatment was not given toward the other two classes, the mummies that have been discovered have greatly increased our knowledge of ancient Egyptian history.

Chapter Two: The Egyptian Gods and Goddesses

Although it is now called mythology, ancient Egyptians used their beliefs as one would practice religion in the present day. As a result, they were well-known for their use of iconography, deities, magic, and human bodies with animal heads.

The mythology of Egypt was the structure of their culture between 4000 BCE through 30 BCE. The death of gods and goddesses as a religion came with Cleopatra, the last ruler of the Ptolemaic Dynasty in Egypt.

Ancient Egypt was formed by the stories and myths that were told about the gods and goddesses. These stories included the creation of the world, the sustaining of their present-day, health, medicine, and more. Mythology also influenced other cultures by the way of the trade market and the opening of the Silk Road in 130 BCE.

By the Silk Road came an important commercial trade between Alexandria and the Egyptian ports. This connection allowed Egyptian tales to become more widespread throughout the world and help other cultures develop the concept of eternal life, life after death, benevolent deities, and reincarnation.

Plato and Pythagoras, two philosophers and mathematicians, found influence in the Egyptian mythological beliefs in reincarnation. Early Rome also borrowed many aspects of religious culture from Egypt.

Characteristics of Egyptian Mythology

There are several key beliefs and aspects that defined Egyptian mythology, such as:

- There were many gods and goddesses (making them polytheistic in nature).

- They had very specific funeral rights.

- The sun was the god of creation.

- There were many animals considered sacred.

- Soul surpassed death if their body was preserved properly.

- Embalming and mummification were used to ensure the soul would move on.

- Many gods had temples.

- They believed in iconography.

Represented Symbolism

There were several symbols that represented specific characteristics of Egyptian life and mythology:

- **Amenhotep** – the architect of sciences, mysteries, and rites. He was not a god, but lived in their time.

- **Ankh** – the symbol of eternal life. It was said that when you put an ankh in your mouth, you breathed life into someone, which was needed for life after death. The ankh means eternity, infinity, or transcendence.

- **Anubis** – the creator of embalming and funeral rites. Anubis had the head of a jackal and the body of a man with dark skin.

- **Dung Beetle** – creation and birth. The dung beetle is related to the sun's cycles of life and the movement around the earth.

- **Eb** – as the god of the cold, he represented the abyss and watery depths.

- **Isis** – as the first daughter of Geb and Nut, Isis taught women how to grind grain, heal, be a homemaker and mother, and spin. Isis represents motherhood, heaven, and wifehood.

- **Maat and her pen** – the symbol of truth, justice, and integrity. Maat was a goddess with wings that represented the stability of the cosmos. She would bring harmony and consistent equilibrium.

- **Nekhbet** – the goddess of water and flight. She had a vulture head with a human body. She flew over Upper Egypt with a ring or royal emblem.

- **Osiris** – the god of vegetation, life, sun personification, and the cosmos. Many people viewed Osiris as the god of civilization. The main temple for his worship was in Heliopolis.

- **Ra** – the sun god, who represented force, life, and power. He was also responsible for death, life, and resurrection. Ra had the head of a hawk and a sacred staff. His symbol was the sun.

- **Shen** – brought eternity as a hoop held by strings. This signifies that there is no beginning or end, and also represents care and protection.

Monsters and Supernatural Creatures

The lower-class people of ancient Egypt had demigods and supernatural creatures, but all myths had monsters to learn lessons from. For example, the sphinx had a man's head with a lion's body and is one of the most commonly recognized creatures in Egyptian mythology.

Amenait, a creature who was strong and furious, lived in the Nile. He had the torso of a hippopotamus, the claws of a lion, the jaw of a crocodile, and a reptile's tail.

Apophis wanted to break the cosmic order. He was an indestructible serpent.

Bennu was a bird who was associated with creation, death, and the sun. The myth was that Bennu burst from the heart of Osiris.

Famous Myths

Since there are over a thousand deities, it would only be right to have that many (and more) stories involving these deities. Some of the more well-known myths are "The Apis Ox" and "Isis and the Seven Scorpions Seek Seth."

In "The Apis Ox," people found a black ox with a white spot on its forehead and a crescent shape on its right side. These facts led people to believe that the ox was actually Osiris, or at least that his soul was in the black ox. Because of this belief, people began worshiping the ox, which also included being fed and served by women, who were the only ones with the right to see him. Eventually, the ox was carried to Memphis where priests took it into the stables and watched where it chose to be in the stables (where it chose to stay became an omen for the Egyptians).

"Isis and the Seven Scorpions Seek Seth" is a tale about revenge, anger, and guilt. As Isis went to find Seth to get revenge with her scorpions, they came to a home in need of shelter for the night. However, the woman chose to not help Isis and her scorpions. Insulted, the scorpions gave a fatal blow to the woman's son. However, Isis, filled with guilt, knew that an innocent man should not die and helped fix the situation.

Gods and Goddesses

Amun – (sometimes seen as Amon) was worshipped as the creator god and is known as the patron god for the city of Thebes. When the two lands unified, he gained more importance as he fused with the sun god Ra. After the unification, Ra and Amun were called Amun-Ra or Amon-Ra.

Amunet – (sometimes referred to as Imnt) is a primordial goddess and Amun's counterpart. She was part of the Ogdoad pantheon and came into popularity (again) in the 20th century when Hollywood used her as an Egyptian queen. However, she is one of the oldest goddesses known in Egypt.

Anubis – the god of the dead, embalming, funerals, and tombs. He was the original god of the underworld, but Osiris replaced him on the throne. Anubis is generally shown with the head of a jackal and the body of a man.

Babi – the god of sexual aggression and the underworld. He was often depicted as a baboon and was called the god of the wild baboons. His name translates to the "bull of baboons" or the "chief baboon."

Bastet – a goddess with a cat or lion's head. She was the protector of the home and the goddess of sensual pleasure. She was the daughter of Ra and Isis and was a very popularly worshiped deity.

Bes – played a number of roles as a minor god. He can be found as the god of war, protector of households, music, dancing, and merriment. He was often referred to as a demigod and is commonly shown as a dwarf with long arms.

Geb – the god of the earth. His parents were Shu and Nut who were the first two gods in the creation myth. Geb was symbolized as the earth, while Nut (the goddess of the sky) was always above him.

Hathor – the goddess of love, beauty, and femininity. She was one of the most famous deities and was often depicted with horns from a cow or a cow's head.

Horus – the god of falcons, skies, and war. Horus would look down at earth and watch over Egypt. He specifically protected the pharaohs.

Isis – the goddess of healing, magic, marriage, and protection. Like Hathor, she can be found with cow horns. Unlike Hathor, Isis has a solar disc between the horns. She is known as the mother of Horus the Younger.

Kek/Kauket – the personification of darkness. They were both female and male and represented night and day. Kek would wear the head of a snake while his female side, Kauket, had the head of a cat or a frog.

Khonsu – the god of the moon in ancient Egypt. He was the son of the goddess Mut and Amun. He is the traveler who is thought to journey the night sky. Like Thoth, he marked time for Egyptians.

Ma'at – the goddess of harmony, justice, and truth. She is one of the most important deities in Egyptian mythology. She embodied the principle of *ma'at*, which is the heart of ancient Egyptian culture. She is represented in the form of the Feather of Truth during the judgment of the soul and continues to be a presence in the Field of Reeds. Her name translates to "that which is straight," and can be found in images as a woman wearing a crown with an ostrich feather.

Menhit – goddess of war with a lioness' head and royal helmet. Menhit means "she who massacres." She was known as the crown goddess when she was adopted into Egyptian mythology. There were times when pharaohs wanted her protection instead of the cobra protection of Uraeus, and they bore the symbol on her crown instead.

Mut – depicted as a lion or a vulture, Mut was a primordial goddess who rose to power in the New Kingdom. She had several attributes from many deities. She is also viewed as a creator.

Nekhbet – the first local goddess with the head of a vulture. She was the goddess of Upper Egypt and one of the most honored deities even after the unification of Egypt. She is the goddess of the dead and the protector of any pharaohs.

Nephthys – the goddess of air and the daughter of Nut and Geb. She was the goddess of protection and cared for souls as their bodies began to die.

Nut – the goddess of the sky. She was represented as a human with a cow's head or shown as a cow in hieroglyphics. Other images will show her arching over her husband, Geb.

Osiris – one of the most popular and prayed to gods. He was the god of creation and then moved to the underworld to give rebirth and afterlife to the souls who deserved it.

Ptah – a deity of craftsmen and architects and also married to Sekhmet. He is thought to have fathered Imhotep and Nefertem. There is a reference of Ptah in many instances as he is known as the lord of truth and eternity, the master of justice, the begetter of the first beginning, and more. He was also believed to have existed before the world itself and thought the world into being.

Ra – the creator of gods and goddesses, he is the sun god. Ra created Bastet, Hathor, Shu, Tefnut, and Sekhmet. When he created them, he did so as the Eye of Ra.

Sekhmet – a lion goddess who was part of the Eye of Ra. When people were disloyal to Ra or when Ra became angry, he would send Sekhmet to kill and slaughter them. However, as fierce as she was when she was angry, when she was calm, she was known as Hathor.

Sobek – the god of rivers and reptiles. Sobek can be found with a man's body and a crocodile's head. Other depictions of crocodiles would also often represent him. He was a fearsome god who no one wanted to upset. However, pharaohs tended to worship him as a military deity as well as the god of fertility. Some legends say that all the world's rivers are made from Sobek's sweat.

Taweret – a goddess who was the protector of pregnancy and motherly care. She often appeared as an upright female hippo who wore Egyptian royal headgear and could scare off evil spirits who came during pregnancy and childbirth. She is thought to be paired with Bes.

Thoth – the god of the moon and knowledge. He was often shown as a man with the head of an ibis (a long-winged and beaked bird). He was married to Ma'at, and they lived on Ra's solar barge to travel throughout the sky with him. Thoth was never a chief in Egypt's pantheon, but was a vital god in all Egyptian mythology.

Wadjet – the patron deity of Lower Egypt, Wadjet was a serpent goddess and was generally shown with the head of a snake. Pharaohs in Lower Egypt would wear her symbol, the cobra (Uraeus), on their crowns for protection. Uraeus and the Eye of Ra were the two symbols that stayed on the crowns after Egypt's unification to pay homage to Wadjet.

Conclusion

Egypt's mythology was once looked at by ancient Egyptians as their religion which was also the structure for everything in their life between 4000 BCE and 30 BCE. Their religion turned into mythology with the death of Cleopatra, who was the last ruler of the Ptolemaic Dynasty in Egypt.

Ancient Egyptian mythologies told stories and myths about gods and goddesses who influenced the creation of the world, built temples, marketed and traded goods, and more. The characteristics of these deities include the sun as the creator of the universe, life after death, sacred animals, mummification, temples, iconography, harmony, and justice.

Because the people held so heartily onto iconography (the worship of statues and symbols), symbols played an enormous part in daily life. These symbols include, but are not limited to: the ankh, Anubis, the dung beetle, a cobra, ostrich feathers, and more.

Monsters and supernatural creatures were more highly acknowledged by the middle and lower classes. These beings would be feared and worshipped locally, but not usually at the state or the national level. One such creature was Amenait, a monster who was made out of the torso of a hippopotamus, the claws of a lion, the jaws of a crocodile, and a reptile's tail, and he lived in the Nile river. Another creature was Apophis, an indestructible snake whose main goal was to disrupt the order of the cosmos.

The myths of Egyptian mythology are far and wide with several thousand deities with stories associated with all of them. The tale of creation, and the tale of Osiris and Set are two of the most popular. Creation began in a swirling darkness of chaos, a pool of endless dark water with no form or purpose. Osiris and Set's story is one of brotherly envy and revenge. It changes the pantheon of the entire universe.

The importance of *ma'at* in Egyptian mythology can be looked at as though it is the foundation of everything that they believed in. *Ma'at* represents harmony, justice, and restoration. The standard myth has two themes of *ma'at*:

1) the disruption of harmony

2) the restoration of harmony (by a hero)

The gods and goddesses are large in stature and numbers. They were so many in number that adding them all to the list would be near impossible. However, there were quite a few popular gods and goddesses that were revered on the local, state, and national level.

Chapter Three: Worshipping the Gods and Goddesses

Ancient Egyptians had a world that revolved around their mythology. They would do whatever was needed to keep their gods and goddesses happy, including rituals, incense, offerings, sacrifices, and more. Large temples and statues were built for worship by the elite classes. Each city in Egypt of the Predynastic Era also had local deities that they worshipped in relation to their occupations as well.

The lower classes would provide offerings of food and flowers during every ceremony to do their part. Other offerings like animal sacrifices and mummies were given to appease the needs and desires of their deities (if required). The animals that were sacrificed were bred and raised solely for the purpose of sacrificing.

Although they were not normally allowed to go to the temples, the people who lived in the middle class and lower classes would be able to build shrines in their homes in order to worship and offer appropriate items. The most popular deities whose shrines were found in various households were that of Taweret and Bes. Ra (the sun god) was also worshipped state-wide.

Temples of Worship

Temples of worship were built as homes to the gods and goddesses. The people believed that the spirit of the gods and goddesses resided inside the statues, which was one reason that the statues were always surrounded by offerings.

Historians can trace the timeline back to 3500 BCE to find some of the earliest temples built. Initially, these temples were made from reeds and wood, but as innovation grew, wooden temples were replaced with stone structures. These temples were generally at the heart of each city throughout the Nile region.

Over time, the temples became more and more elaborate. The Egyptians aligned their temples to their environment and to go along with the movement of the sun and stars. Each temple's place became a sacred space, which was then encircled by a mud wall. Inside the mud wall, people would find a series of stone buildings and courtyards where each building would be dedicated to a different god or goddess.

Eventually, the temple walls were decorated with murals of brightly colored scenes of the gods and goddesses and their stories. The depiction of stories would soon carry over to floors and ceilings as well. However, instead of paint, Egyptians used an inlay of precious metals (like gold and silver) and gemstones for decoration.

To add more importance to the temples, toward the center, the rooms would become smaller and darker until the innermost center. Here is where the statues resided. These statues were kept in a way to show reverence to their spirits (which lived inside the statues). They were maintained with daily rituals, cleanings, and offerings to satisfy any desire of the gods and goddesses.

Priests presided over the temple to make sure that the deities were taken care of in the proper way. The temples became a powerhouse of divinity that would then redirect that power throughout the rest of the country for their benefit.

Because the spaces had to be kept pure, only clergy and royals were allowed to enter them. The temple's outer areas did allow middle- and lower-class people to enter for worship, close to the administrative buildings.

The temples became the epicenter of each town. They housed the religious centers, town halls, libraries, universities, medical centers, and courts of law. These were all places where people came together for community life and to be closer to the gods and goddesses.

Celebrations

Holidays are not a new idea from the last century. Many cultures have created reasons to celebrate since the first historical documents were found. Ancient Egyptians were no exception; they had several celebrations throughout the year that would coincide with a god or goddess.

The **Egyptian New Year** began the celebrational season off. It was considered the opening of the year and was celebrated on July 19th (month one, day one of the Egyptian calendar). This date would represent the beginning of the annual Nile River flood. This flood would bring water to the farms and allow for healthy growing crops. The floodwaters were a time of national rejoicing. People threw flowers, offerings, and themselves into the water.

The **Opet Festival** happened in what we know as September, which was the second month on days 15 through 26 in the Egyptian calendar. The Opet Festival was an 11-day event where the statue of Amun would be taken out of its temple with a parade of dancers, soldiers, musicians, and the public. The procession would travel south for five kilometers (3.10 miles) to a new temple where the statue would be joined by the pharaoh who performed secret ceremonies that would replenish their royal power. Meanwhile, those outside would feast and rejoice.

The **Festival of Khoiak** would happen in the fourth month between days 18 and 30 in the Egyptian calendar (which would be what we know as November). The festival would celebrate the life, death, and resurrection of Osiris, and would be represented by the agricultural cycle where the crops were harvested and ready to grow again. Ceremonies included planting seeds in containers that were shaped like Osiris. The celebration would happen during the receding times of the Nile floodwaters when the soil would be rich and black. This texture and color would mean that the soil was ready for new crops to be planted.

The **Festival of Bastet** is held in the eighth month between days 4 and 5. This festival was centered around fertility and celebrated with singing, dancing, and drinking. Everyone would come to the center of Bubastis for the festival where more wine would be drunk at the feast than any other time of the year. Goddesses Bastet, Sekhmet, and Hathor would be worshiped during this time.

The **Festival of the Valley** would be celebrated at the time of the new moon in the 10th month. This festival was an annual celebration where the statue of Amun would be taken from Karnak to Thebes on the west bank, which was across the Nile River. People would take the statue to visit other tombs, temples, and buried kings. The public was also invited to visit the relatives who had passed on and given the chance to feast with their spirits and provide them offerings.

The **Festival of the Beautiful** was celebrated in the eleventh month on the day of the new moon. This festival was in memory of the marriage between the god Horus of Edfu and the goddess Hathor of Dendera. Fourteen days before the new moon, priests would move

Hathor's cult statue 70 kilometers (43.5 miles) and place it beside the statue of Horus. The next two weeks would be full of festivities that involved both royalty and the local people.

Servants of Gods

In ancient Egypt, the religious focus was led by priests, who instead of calling themselves priests, pastors, or monks, were called "servants of gods." These people would initiate and carry out religious rites before the statues in each temple.

The only people allowed to go into the temples were the servants of gods and the child of the gods (aka, each new pharaoh). Since there was only one pharaoh, they would delegate the temples that needed to be worshipped to the priest in the highest rank, who would then scatter the duties to other clergy members. Each member of the high priest rank would be selected by each new pharaoh. These priests would usually be a relative of noble blood, which could also promote loyalty.

In larger temples such as at Karnak or Memphis, the temple treasures were abundant, and the amount of land tended to be considerable. These details made those high priest positions especially prestigious due to the extent of power and wealth associated with them.

These priests would control the statues, who acted as the mouthpiece of each god. The statues were known to be oracles, and the priests would interpret their pronouncements, pass judgment in legal cases, and could point to a new royal successor.

There were other times, especially when the crown was at its weakest, that the high priest's power became greater than the pharaoh's, and they took on more roles. One of these roles could lead to civil wars because they would take on the responsibility of a military general. In heartier times, the priest would carry out their role of taking care of the gods, their spirits, and maintaining relations.

There were female and male clergy members who helped the high priest lead daily rituals in homage to the god or goddess of that temple. There were many roles that the clergy filled, including the "god's wife." Priestesses and lector priests who were literate would read sacred texts while others would become like astronomers, temple dancers, singers, musicians, etc.

The temples had other staff including the gardeners, brewers, bakers, butchers, and more. These staff members would supply daily offerings, weave temple garments, create jewelry, cut hair, make wigs, craft statues, build structures, and maintain the temple.

There were times when the number of people who worked in the temples was over 100,000 people, which was the case at each of the three main temples in Heliopolis, Karnak, and Memphis.

Women as Priestesses

Being a woman did not stop you from being a priestess to either a god or a goddess. Priestesses were also paid the same amount of money as their male counterparts, and they did the same amount and kind of work.

The priestess title that was commonly used was "chantress." These women would act out the goddess in rituals. Another common title was the "leader of the musical troupe." As for the role of the high priest, history shows that there were more men than women who took on the role, but that there were women who did as well.

However, the most important role a woman could become was the "god's wife." This title was held by royal women who acted as a consort for the god Amun at Karnak. The god's wife took part in sacred processions with only the pharaoh and the high priest. These processions generally took place at the innermost shrine. God's wife would make offerings and keep each god content. She defended Egypt by magical means as she shot arrows into ritual targets and would burn images of enemies.

Like the high priest, god's wife would be appointed by the pharaoh. These appointees would usually be the sister or daughter of the pharaoh, which would enhance their status as well. They would be regarded as an equal to the pharaoh, and if ever needed, they would be able to delegate responsibilities on the king's behalf in state and temple matters.

Conclusion

The world of ancient Egypt revolved around their religion. They worked daily to keep their gods and goddesses happy by building large temples and statues to worship them. People who were in lower classes would give offerings of food and flowers during each ceremony throughout the year.

Temples of worship were homes built for the gods and the goddesses. The oldest temple found was built around 3500 BCE.

At first, the temples were made from wood and reeds, but over time they became elaborate cities that had over 100,000 people tending to them every day. These buildings were stone structures that had courtyards and buildings dedicated to a different god or goddess.

Walls were constructed around the temples so that there was an inner area and an outer area. Murals of the gods and goddesses performing magic or taking part in one of their stories were painted with bright colors, inlaid with metals, and decorated with gemstones.

Priests and priestesses would preside over the temples with only the head priest and his assistants allowed to tend to the needs of the gods and goddesses. The only other person allowed into the inner sanctuary of the temple would be the pharaohs.

There were many celebrations where the statues of the gods and goddesses were moved. Some were moved only a couple of miles while others were moved up to forty miles, all for the sake of worship and ritual.

Men and women were both allowed to be servants of the gods. Each had a title and a role in the clergy. They also were paid similarly. The highest roles they could be were that of the high priest or the god's wife. All roles were made to please the gods and the goddesses, whether it be to maintain the gardens in the outer areas of the temple or to be known as the god's wife and become the consort of a god.

Chapter Four: Famous Stories from Egyptian Mythology

Stories were part of the entire Egyptian diaspora. The people learned lessons, values, morals, and strived to keep daily life in *ma'at*. Although iconography played such a huge role in the celebrations, rituals, government, and clergy, the stories about their gods and goddesses were at the heart of their religion.

Some of the most famous stories include the "Creation Story," "Osiris, Isis, & Set," "Horus & Set," "The Seven Year Famine," "The Greek Princess," "The Doomed Prince," "The Golden Lotus," "The Princess of Bekhten," "The Peasant and the Workman," "Ma'at," "The Goddess of Morality," and many more.

In this chapter we will cover some of the most popular myths told even to this day.

Creation

The Egyptian mythology creation story began when the universe burst out of swirling darkness and chaos. It all starts with a pool of water that is endless and dark. The water has no form or purpose.

However, Heka, the god of magic, existed within the void and waited for the moment of creation. Nu, the water silence, rose a primordial hill (*ben-ben*) with Atum (or Ptah) who stood on top.

Atum looked over the vast nothingness and realized how alone he was. With his magic and his shadow, he gave birth to two children: Shu, the god of air (spat out by his father), and Tefnut, the goddess of moisture (who was vomited out by Atum). Shu gave the world the principles of life while Tefnut gave order to principles.

After principles of life and the principles of order were created, Shu and Tefnut left their father at the *ben-ben* and went to establish the world. Fearing that they were gone too long, Atum removed his eye and sent it off to search for them. As he waited for his eye and his children to return, he began to think about eternity. Once his children and his eye returned, he shed tears of joy. These tears fertilized the ground under the *ben-ben*, which gave birth to men and women.

Since men and women had no place to live, Shu and Tefnut mated to give birth to Geb (the earth) and Nut (the sky). Although Geb and Nut were brother and sister, they fell deeply in love and became inseparable.

Seeing this as unacceptable, Atum pushed the earth and the sky high into the heavens away from each other where they could forever be able to see but never touch one another. However, Nut, already pregnant with five children from Geb, soon gave birth to Osiris, Horus, Isis, Nephthys, and Set.

These gods and goddesses are recognized as the earliest and most familiar representation of god-heads in Egyptian mythology.

Osiris, Isis, and Set

Atum saw that Osiris was a just and responsible ruler. In this light, Atum made Osiris the supreme ruler of the world and decreed that everyone should answer to him. However, Osiris co-ruled the world with his sister-wife, Isis.

Together, they chose the best trees to grow in the best places and decided where the water would be the sweetest. Osiris created the land of Egypt in perfect harmony with the Nile River to provide everything that the people would need.

Osiris honored his siblings by keeping things in balance. He used the principle of *ma'at* (harmony) to guide him. He did so well that his brother Set grew jealous of his power and what he and Isis created.

When the time came, Set had Osiris's measurements taken in secret and ordered an elaborate chest to be created. Once the chest was made, Set invited Osiris and 72 other people to a great banquet. The prize at the end of the night was the chest. Set would give the chest to anyone who could fit inside. This treachery was made possible by the fact that Osiris fit perfectly inside the chest.

After Osiris climbed into the chest, Set locked the lid on and threw it into the Nile River. Set then announced that his brother was dead and took control of the world.

Isis refuted the death claims and went searching for Osiris. She found the chest up a tree in the city of Byblos, where the people were happy to help get the coffin down. Isis blessed the people of the town and from that time, the city was an important location of papyrus export and a great staple for the writer's trade.

Isis then brought her husband's body back to Egypt. She hid his body away until she could gather herbs to make a potion, which would bring her husband back to life. Her sister, Nephthys, was charged with guarding the hiding place of Osiris' body.

During the time Isis was searching for Osiris' body, Set began to worry about what would happen if she did find it and bring him back to life (Isis was extremely educated in these matters). When he saw that she was gone, Set went to his other sister Nephthys and asked where Isis was. Nephthys gave Set an answer, but Set knew that she was lying.

He used force and cunningness to get Osiris' body from Nephthys. He then cut Osiris' body into 42 pieces (although the number is debated, as some reference the number 14) and tossed the pieces throughout Egypt, ensuring that Isis would not be able to find them all. Satisfied, Set went back to the palace to rule once again.

When Isis returned, she found the coffin destroyed and Osiris' body gone. She wept in despair. Nephthys, guilty from her betrayal, helped Isis concoct a plan that would find the body parts of Osiris. The sisters started on their quest and whenever they found a part of Osiris, they collected it and built a shrine over the piece to protect it from Set. This action is said to be how the 42 provinces of Egypt were established.

When all of the pieces of Osiris' body were found, they realized that his penis was missing because it was eaten by a fish. Isis molded a new phallus, he was revived, and they made love together. Through this interaction, she became pregnant with her son, Horus.

Although Osiris was brought back to life, he was still incomplete and could not rule the world as he once did. Instead, he went to rule the underworld where he became the righteous judge and ruler of the dead.

Horus (or Horus the Younger) was raised in secret. Isis was fearful of what Set would do to her son if he ever found out about him. Once Horus the Younger grew into manhood, he challenged Set for the throne of Egypt. The battle lasted eight years until, finally, Horus won.

Horus then banished Set from Egypt who now would have to roam the arid deserts (or depending upon the version of the story, was destroyed, or chose to divide the kingdom in two). Horus ruled with his mother and aunt as his counselors with peace and harmony restored to Egypt.

The Mythical Murder Pot: Set & Horus

When Horus challenged Set to the throne, a series of battles began. While the war waged on for many years, due to Set's devious ways, he continued to win the smaller battles.

Furious with her brother, Isis decided to step in to help her son. She set a trap for Set and caught him. When she was ready to take her final blow, Set began begging for his life. In that moment of vulnerability, Isis let him go.

Horus was so furious that his anger even upset the other gods. In the final match, a boat race, it looked as though Horus was to be the winner. As Set never played fair, he turned into a hippopotamus and attacked Horus' boat. This then turned into another battle.

In the end, after the long years of battle, Horus and Set turned to Osiris and asked him who should be the king. Osiris declared that anyone who receives a throne through murderous ways should not be king, just as Set had done. And so, Horus took his rightful place on the throne, and Osiris continued to rule the underworld.

Ma'at, the Goddess of Morality

As the goddess of truth, justice, harmony, and morality, she weighed the hearts of the dead to see who should have joy in the eternity of the afterlife. She was also the daughter of Ra and the wife of the moon god, Thoth.

When she used the Feather of Truth, it would determine whose heart was heavier than her feather. If placed on the scale and the heart was heavier, they would not be allowed to enter the Field of Reeds.

However, if their heart was too heavy, a demon would devour it. The demon would then push the deceased into the death of nothing, as they felt death the second time.

The Death Myth for Anubis

Anubis was mainly known as the god of death. Once Osiris gained popularity, Anubis was pushed from the title of "lord of the dead," to the son of Osiris who was his helper in the afterlife.

Anubis protected tombs and invented mummification. He would oversee the weighing of the heart and would take dead souls to the underworld for their final judgment.

The Book of Thoth

This book held all the knowledge of the gods and goddesses. There was a locked series of boxes in the Nile that was guarded by snakes. This knowledge was coveted by many pharaohs who could never open it in their reigns. This was because this knowledge was never meant to be known by mortals, which could be the way ancient Egyptians explained many uncertainties.

However, the box is still said to lay at the bottom of the Nile River.

The Girl with the Rose-Red Slippers

This concept could be where the story of Cinderella began. A young, Greek girl was captured and sold into slavery in Egypt. A very kind man purchased her and lavished amazing gifts on her after their return to his home.

One day, an eagle flew by and saw her wearing the rose-red slippers. He swooped down to steal one of them and delivered it to the pharaoh, Amasis.

Amasis asked the eagle to take him to the owner of the slipper. When the Greek girl and Amasis met, it was love at first sight. They loved each other so deeply that they even died on the same day.

A God Who Saved Princess Bekhten

While a pharaoh was collecting his annual tributes in Nehern, the Prince of Bekhten presented him with his eldest daughter, Ra-neferu. Taken with her, the pharaoh accepted the princess and brought her back to Egypt. Ra-neferu became his chief, royal wife.

Many years later, Ra-neferu's sister, Bent-Reshet, became very ill. The Prince of Bekhten sent word of her illness and asked the pharaoh for help. Even though the pharaoh sent a physician, he determined that the illness was caused by an evil spirit and he would not be able to help. The pharaoh then went to the temple of Khonsu Nefer-hetep to ask the god for help healing Bent-Reshet.

The god, hearing the pharaoh's plea came down to Egypt and confronted the evil spirit, which caused it to leave Bent-Reshet. Being a little foolish, the pharaoh tried to keep the powerful god, Khonsu, in Bekhten in the hope that other great things would come from the god's presence.

But, after three years, the pharaoh realized how he behaved and released the god back into the heavens. Feeling so guilty for his actions, the pharaoh began setting offerings and gifts at the feet of Khonsu's statue in the Great Temple.

The Seven Year Famine

This myth is a story of how Khnemu saves Egypt from the ravages that a seven-year-long famine befell on the people.

King Tcheser, the third king of a third dynasty, sent a dispatcher to Mater (the high official who ruled the region of the South, the Island of Elephantine, and the district of Nubia) to say that he was in grief in his eighteenth year.

His grief was caused by how he was brought to sit on the throne and in his last seven years as pharaoh, the Nile River had not been inundated in a satisfactory way. The lack of water caused a famine for the people as grain, vegetables, and garden produce became scarce.

Chaos was starting to ensue with his people. Neighbors were robbing one another for food, men were so weak they could no longer walk, children were crying out in hunger, and elders were just laying down to die where they stood.

In response, Mater responded to the king by coming to him quickly. He promised to help, as he knew that the Nile flood came from the first city that ever existed, the Island of Elephantine. Mater then told the king to seek help from the god, Khnemu.

When the king heard this news, he offered up many gifts and sacrifices to the god Khnemu at his temple. After much time, Khnemu appeared before the pharaoh. He said, "I am the Creator. My hand rests upon you to protect you and make your body sound. I will give you my heart. I am he, who created myself . . ."

When Khnemu heard the king's pleas and saw the sacrifices and gifts the pharaoh left for him, Khnemu promised the Nile will rise every year as it once did. As an homage, King Tcheser set out a decree that one side of the Nile, near Elephantine, would be sacred to Khnemu and that part of the land would house a temple dedicated to Khnemu. A tax would also be levied on every product of the neighborhood that would be devoted only to the maintenance of his shrine.

Land of the Dead

Only two people have ever traveled to Duat, the land of the dead, and returned alive to tell the tale.

Se-Osiris, a wonderful child magician, and his father, Setna, stood at the window of the palace in Thebes and watched two funerals. The first funeral was for a rich man, who was mummified and laid to rest in a wooden case lined with gold. Troops and mourners carried him to the burial site and priests walked around in the front and back of his body chanting and singing hymns.

The second funeral was for a poor man who worked as a laborer. His two sons carried his simple wooden case with his widow and daughters-in-law as his only mourners.

Setna, the son of Pharaoh Rameses, watched the two funerals and said, "I hope that my fate will be that of the rich noble, and not of the poor laborer."

Se-Osiris contradicted him and said, "I pray that the poor man's fate may be yours and not that of the rich man."

Setna became confused and hurt by his son's words, and seeing this, Se-Osiris tried to explain himself. "Whatever you see in this funeral procession matters very little. What does matter is your judgment with Osiris. Let me prove it to you. If you trust yourself to me, I know the words to open the gates to the Judgment Hall of Osiris. I can release your *Ba* (soul) and mine. Then we can fly into *Duat* (the world of the dead), and see what happens there. It is when you see what goes on that you may change your view of what the fates should give you. The rich man may have worked in evil during his life, and the poor man may have done nothing but good."

Setna knew that his child had wonderful gifts and trusted his son. So, he agreed to go with Se-Osiris, even though he was afraid they may not be able to return.

Father and son made their way to the temple of Osiris. When they arrived, Se-Osiris began the ritual and said the words to open the gate and to release their *Ba*.

Setna soon realized he was no longer in his body and heard his son say, "Follow me now, father. We must leave now and be back by sunset if we are to live to see another day."

Setna turned to where his son's voice came from to see a beautiful bird with gold feathers and the head of his son. "I'll follow now."

Setna watched as the world of Egypt and the tomb melted away. They found themselves in the First Region. Six serpents were curled on either side of the golden towing boat as they floated along the ghostly river of death. The Second Region was in the Kingdom of Re. Here were the villages that gods and heroes lived in; they were guarded by spirits of the corn who made the wheat and barley plentiful in the growing season.

As the golden boat floated over, they then sailed through the Third Region and stopped at the judgment hall of Osiris. Although many spirits and *Ba* exited the boat, many others sailed on to the other nine regions of the night.

Setna and Se-Osiris left the boat along with those who were going to the hall of judgment. Se-Osiris gave the doorman his name and was shuffled in along with the rest of the souls to be judged. They watched men and women proclaim their purity, but their hearts and the Feather of Truth told the true story.

Soon, came the rich man and the poor man.

Anubis took out the heart of the wealthy man and added it to the scale. He then placed the feather of truth on the other side. The heart of the rich man showed to be a heavy heart, as it pulled the scale down until it sank so low that Ammit the Devourer opened the floor up, and pulled the evil man away with his jaws.

However, when the poor man gave his heart, it was the feather that sank down and his heart that rose, showing the audience that he was a good man. Horus took the pure man who had done no sinning and gave him bread and beer. The dead man rejoiced, took his food and drink, and followed Horus to the Field of Reeds.

Surprised, Setna turned to his son, who said, "Now you know why I wished your fate to be that of the poor man."

Setna understood. He held onto his son's back as the Ba spread its golden wings to fly them home. They entered their bodies just in time to see the sunrise.

Isis and the Seven Scorpions

This tale is about Isis, who managed to gain even more magic than she had originally.

After the murder of Osiris and the issues with Set, Isis went into hiding with her son to avoid something perilous happening to him. Everywhere she went, she was accompanied by seven scorpions.

Three of the scorpions, Peter, Tjetet, and Matet walked in front of her to make sure that her path was safe. At either side were Mesetet and Mesetetef, and walking behind her, and watching her back, were Tefen and Befen.

Each night, Isis warned any companions to avoid speaking with anyone and to avoid alerting Set to where they were. However, one night, when Isis was traveling to the town of Two Sisters in the Nile Delta, a noblewoman saw a woman (Isis) who was surrounded by scorpions arrive. The woman became frightened, and she quickly shut the door to her house.

Enraged by her rude behavior, the scorpions decided to teach the woman a lesson. Tefen loaded his stinger with the poison of the six other scorpion companions while Isis found refuge with a peasant girl in her simple home.

The scorpions were not swayed from their anger at the noblewoman, no matter how much the girl's kindness to Isis they saw. And, in retaliation, Tefen snuck out of the house, crawled under the door, and stung the noblewoman's son. Distraught, the woman knocked on each person's door in the town, hoping to find help for her child who was now about to die.

Isis heard the woman's cries and although the woman did display unkindness to her, Isis could not let someone's son die. Isis left with the woman, and they went to go help her son.

When they got back to her house, Isis held the boy in her arms and spoke great magical words. She named each of the scorpions, reclaimed their poison from the child, and rendered the combined poison harmless to him.

Humbled by Isis and her unconditional kindness, the noblewoman offered everything in her possession to Isis and the peasant girl who had shown hospitality to a stranger.

The Golden Lotus

The 4th Dynasty was very magical, and this story may sound familiar to the parting of the Red Sea.

The great pyramid of Giza was built by Pharaoh Khufu. His father, Seneferu, had ruled over Egypt through a long period of contentment and peace. When Seneferu reigned, there were no foreign wars and few troubles at home.

However, with so little to do in the matter of state, he often found himself with a lot of time on his hands. Bored and wandering, Seneferu walked through his Memphis palace trying to find something to lighten his heart.

He went to his chief magician, Zazamankh, and asked if anyone was able to show him something new. He said, "I have searched throughout my palace for some delight and found none. Please give me your wisdom and devise something to fill my heart with pleasure."

The chief magician told him to go sailing on the Nile River and follow it to the lake below Memphis. "Although it is no common voyage, you will come across many marvelous things."

With some doubt, Seneferu ordered his royal boat be brought to him. Zazamankh assured him, again, that the voyage would be something new, and unexpected. The first new thing would be that Seneferu's rowers would be different from anyone he had seen before.

Instead, Seneferu would have to get maidens from the royal house of the King's Women. Zazamankh then instructed him to watch the women row until they saw the birds on the lake. He would then see the fields and green grass on the banks, and his heart would grow glad.

Seneferu began to get excited at the prospect of something new. He charged the magician with running the expedition and gathering everyone and everything that they would need.

Zazamankh told the pharaoh's attendants to bring him twenty oars of ebony inlaid with gold. The oars should also have blades that were inlaid with electrum. He then wanted twenty of the fairest ladies who were virgins with flowing hair. And lastly, he needed twenty nets made with golden thread. Once the nets were made, they would be worn by the maidens as garments along with other jewelry of electrum and malachite.

When all was done and presented to the pharaoh, they loaded the royal boat and started to go. Seneferu did feel happy watching maidens perform a task they never had before, and he enjoyed being at sea.

But, when the party was on the lake, and the stern was raised, one of the handles of the oars brushed against the head of a girl who was wearing her hair swept up in a golden lotus. She leaned over and looked for her hair decoration.

As she did this, she stopped rowing and singing, and so did the rest of the rowers on her side.

The pharaoh asked, "Why have you stopped rowing?"

The girls replied that their steerer, the girl who lost her golden lotus hair decoration, no longer led them. He turned to the steerer and asked her why she stopped leading.

The girl explained to him that she only wanted her golden lotus decoration and no other. The king tried to sway her otherwise, but she would not be moved. So, he beckoned for the chief magician and explained the situation to Zazamankh.

The chief magician stood at the boat's stern and chanted spells and words of power. He held his hand over the water, and the lake parted as if it had been cut in two by a great sword. The lake was twenty feet deep with walls of water that rose up to forty feet high. The boat began to sink slowly down into the empty space between the water of the walls.

Once the boat made it safely to the ground, they could see the golden lotus decoration uncovered and dry.

The maiden who lost the decoration leaped over the side of the ship to the firm ground and picked it up. She fastened it in her hair and came aboard to once again steer the boat home.

As they sailed home, Zazamankh lowered his hands and the royal boat slid up the water until it was level with the lake's surface again. The walls of water returned to their regular levels and the royal boat continued to sail toward their destination.

On their way home, the maidens sang a song that is native to Egypt:

"She stands upon the further side,

Between us flows the Nile,

And in those waters deep and wide,

There lurks a crocodile.

Yet is my love so true and sweet,

A word of power, a charm,

The stream is land beneath my feet,

And bears me without harm.

For I shall come to where she stands,

No more be held apart.

And I shall take my darling's hands,

And draw her to my heart."

Conclusion

In the previous chapters you have learned about the Ancient Egyptian lifestyle, along with the religion of the time. You have learned about the primary gods that were broadly worshipped across Egypt, and the different stories and myths associated with them.

The Ancient Egyptians were a polytheistic people, worshipping hundreds of different gods. For their time, they were an incredibly advanced society, possessing a wide arrange of knowledge on topics ranging from agriculture, to medicine, to astrology, to construction.

Ancient Egyptian culture and mythology is an ever-evolving field of study, with new findings still being made thousands of years later. While the entire pantheon and history of Ancient Egypt would require dozens of books to properly cover, I hope that you have enjoyed this introduction into Ancient Egypt, what life was like, how the different social classes lived, and how they worshipped their gods.